Book 1

Hacking

By: PG WIZARD BOOKS

&

Book 2

XML Crash Course

By: PG WIZARD BOOKS

Book 1

Hacking

By: PG WIZARD BOOKS

Top Online Handbook in Exploitation of Computer Hacking, Security, and Penetration Testing!

Hacking: Top Online Handbook in Exploitation of Computer Hacking, Security, and Penetration Testing!

Table of Contents

Hacking: Top Online Handbook in Exploitation of Computer Hacking, Security, and Penetration Testing!

Introduction

The world of hacking is an interesting world. Most of us only understand what is going on based on the movies that we watch or the news that we read about hackers stealing identities of those around them. These are parts of the whole hacking world, but there is so much more that comes with it. For example, some hackers are considered ethical hackers, which means that they are going to work to prevent others from getting onto their own systems, or the systems of others they are working for.

This guidebook is going to take some time to discuss the basics of the hacking world. We will start out with the difference between white hat hackers and black hat hackers and how each of them are going to work on the hacks that they are creating. We will then move on to working with how to map out your hack, especially if you want to check for vulnerabilities inside of your own system. And then the rest of the book will spend time looking at some of the common types of hacking that you can do including man in the middle hacks and even hacking passwords.

Even when it comes to hacking into a network that you are allowed to be on, it is important to learn how to do some basic hacks because you will be using the same methods that the black hat hackers are doing as well. This guidebook is going to help you to get started with doing some of the hacks that you need to ensure that you are getting the best results that you want!

Chapter 1: Some of the Basics of Computer Hacking

The process of hacking has gotten a bad name, mainly because of all the stories that have gone on in the media and in the movies about this topic. We may imagine someone who is just trying to get onto a system the are not allowed to be in or about someone who hacks into the government computers in order to get some important information and save the day. But there are many different facets that come up when we are talking about hacking and while some hackers are interested in stealing information and being places they aren't allowed to be, there are some who are more interested in learning hacking in order to protect their own computer systems and information.

There are two main types of computer hacking that you can come across. These include:

- Black hat hacking: this is the type that is found inside the movies. This is when someone tries to get onto a system that they don't belong, without the permission of the person who owns the system. Often this is done so that the hacker is able to get information they are not supposed to have, such as your personal information and credit card numbers.
- White hat hacking: this is the type of hacking that you may do when trying to keep your computer system and information safe from someone who may try to get the information and use it for their own reasons. Also, white hat hackers may also work with a big company, working on hacking on the system to see if it is vulnerable, in order to keep other people out of the system.

Both of these types of hackers are going to use the same methods to do the hacking, but the reasons behind the hacking are going to be completely different. It is important to note that black hat hacking is illegal and if you do this kind of hacking, it could end up with you going to jail and in a lot of trouble. But there is nothing wrong with hacking on to a system that you have permission to be on, such as your own personal computer, to help keep it safe or as part of your job.

Hacking: Top Online Handbook in Exploitation of Computer Hacking, Security, and Penetration Testing!

Penetration testing

Now that we have a little basics of the world of hacking, it is time to look more into the world of computer hacking. We will start this out with penetration testing. This is known as an authorized attempt in order to exploit a computer system in the hopes of learning the flaws that are inside of it so that you can work to make it more secure. When you are given the assignment to do a penetration test, or you decide to do it on your own system, you will be investigating the system in order to prove that there are vulnerabilities in the network.

After you are done with doing the penetration test, the mitigation measures will be made in order to address any of the issues that you found and fix the issues that you discovered during this test. It is basically a process of finding the threats that are present inside of the system and then come up with a good plan that is going to take care of the issues that show up during the test. Doing these on occasion to the system can ensure that you catch the vulnerabilities inside the system before someone else gets on and steals your information.

Penetration testing is also known as ethical hacking. There is a very thin line that is present between vulnerability assessment and penetration testing. These terms are often interchanged but they are not really the same thing. For example, the vulnerability assessment is going to be responsible for evaluations the system for any security issues that may be present already. But the penetration test is going to be the test that is used in order to exploit and also proves that these security issues exist. The test is going to allow the hacker to test out the system as an outside source so that they can see how the vulnerabilities are affecting things.

As a white hat hacker, you would want to go through the system and perform the same actions that a black hat hacker would do on the system in this kind of test. You would try to get onto the system to see how bad the vulnerabilities are and to determine what information others are able to see. While the black hat hacker would simply do this in the hopes of trying to get onto the system and exploit it for their own personal gains, you are going to find out where these things are and learn how to close them up. Even though both of you will use the same methods in order to get onto the system, you are going to have different reasons for getting onto the system.

A hacking lab

As a beginner to working on hacking, you may want to consider working in a hacking lab. This is a safe environment that you are able to work in with the attacks and the traffic to see how they respond to different things that you are working on, without them getting out of hand and heading to places they are not supposed to be. This is a good place for a beginner to get started with because it allows you to get some practice without ruining anything in the system or causing some issues. Once you get a little bit more of the practice into the thing, you will be able to move out of the hacking lab and have some fun with hacking, and do some of the tests, on a real network.

While there are some differences in the reason for hacking between a white hat and a black hat hacker, both of these groups are going to use the same kinds of skills and techniques in order to get the information that they want. The trick here is for the white hat hacker to know just as much, of not more, and to be faster at finding the vulnerabilities compared to the black hat hacker. This will help to keep the system protected and ensures that the other group isn't able to get information they are not supposed to have.

Chapter 2: Mapping Out the Hack Before Beginning

So before we get too far in this process, it is important to come up with the plan that you want to use. This is meant to give you a good idea of what you need to do and where you want to look for some of these vulnerabilities inside of your system. The strategies that you will use are important, but you really need to focus on having a good plan in place before you get too far in this process.

When you are trying to find some of the vulnerabilities that are needed, you don't need to waste your time checking all of the protocols for security at the same time. This can make it a bit confusing and sometimes it is going to make you deal with more problems than you want because too much information is coming towards you. This means that you should break your system up into parts and then test each of these parts so that the work is more manageable overall.

For the most part, it is a good idea to start out with the application or system that you are worried about the most, and then go down the list until you get to each of them. To help you to determine which of the systems you should work with first, consider these questions:

- If the system is attacked, which system or application is going to cause the most issues. Which one has the most information or would be the hardest to fix up if it were lost.
- If the system is attacked, which application is going to be the easiest for the hacker to get in to.
- Which sections of the system are you working on and are considered the least documented, which means that they are rarely checked. Do you notice some that you have never seen there before?

As you answer these questions, it is going to become easier to figure out which applications you should work on first and it is easier to go through the whole process and find the results that you want. There are many places that you are able to check out to make sure the tests are run the proper way including the routers and the switches, workstations and laptops, operating systems, databases and applications, firewalls, files, and emails servers and more. It is possible that you will need to run many tests to get all of these so take your time and try them out to see where the vulnerabilities may lie.

When should I do my hack?

Once you have a good list of the applications and devices that you want to check, the next question that you may have is when is a good time to hack. You will need to make sure that you complete the hacks during a time that is going to cause the least amount of disruption in the company or on your own personal computer. This means during the peak hours of the day, you should not be doing these hacks because they could potentially cause a lot of slow down and issues with the system and depending on the type of hack that you do, and if it goes well or not, it could even shut down the network when it is needed most. The best time to complete the tasks is when there is going to be minimal disruption, so coming in after hours is often best since few people will be on the system or the building could be closed and no one will even notice.

The time that works the best for these hacks will vary depending on the situation. For example, if you are doing one of these hacks on your own computer, the timing may not matter as much because you would just pick a time when you are free to do the hacks and call it good. On the other hand, if you are doing this as a job for your employer, you will need to abide by their busy times and pick one that is not going to interfere with the business, especially if the hack does cause some issues.

Will others see what I am doing?

When you are working on these hacks in order to find some of the vulnerabilities that are in the system, you need to think just like a criminal hacker would, since these are the type of people that would try to get onto the system. Sometimes being able to look at the system through fresh eyes can make all the difference. For example, when you are used to using this system, you are an insider and could have troubles seeing what is going on in the system, but it is important that you make sure that when you do the hacks, no one else is able to see what you are doing. The criminal hacker would be careful about who is able to notice their presence so you would want to be the same way.

Now, it is your job to also check out what the hacker is able to see on your system. Hackers are always trying to find out as much information about the system as possible to make it easier to get onto it, and there are trails left all over the place for them to look at. As the ethical hacker of the system, it is your responsibility to find out what kind of information is out there for the other hackers to find and then learn how to diminish these trails to make your website and system harder to mess with. There are several different scanner types that you are able to use, such as a port scanner, so that you can see what information that is being shared, making it easier to catch some of these issues. Some of the other searches that you can do to protect your network includes doing a search online for the following information:

Any contact details. This is going to be information that can point back to the people connected with your business. Some options like USSearch and ChoicePoint are good ones to visit and see if your information is present there.

Look for any recent press releases that may talk about changes that have happened in the organization.

Look through any of the acquisitions and mergers of the company.

Always see if you can find any SEC documents about the company online.

Any patents or trademarks that are associated with this company.

Incorporation filings. These are also found through the SEC, but sometimes they are located elsewhere.

Be as thorough as possible about this point so that you have a good idea of what hackers are able to find out about your company or about your network. Often doing a keyword search is not going to bring up the results that you would like so you need to work with some advanced searches to find out all the information that you would like. At this point, you have a good idea of the different things that your computer or your network is sending out to other people and you can create the plan to get it all under control. Deleting information from online can help but running some port and network scans are great as well. Go through as many of these scans and tests as you can to help keep the computer network as safe as possible.

Chapter 3: Doing a Spoofing Attack

The first type of attack that we are going to explore is the spoofing attack. Whether you are working as a criminal hacker or as an ethical hacker, there are a lot of things that you can work with in order to get into a system that you shouldn't be on. As a hacker, you are responsible for researching and having some patience to wait in order to find the vulnerability that is on the system or network before taking the next move. But with the right kind of work, it is easier to get on the network and often a few different options are going to show up for you. One method that you can use is the spoofing technique that allows you to convince the computer system that you should be there so that you can get all the information that you want. Let's take a look at how this works and how you can make it happen with your hacking.

Spoofing

One of the first techniques that we are going to explore in this guidebook is spoofing. This is basically going to be a technique where the hacker is able to pretend that they are another person, software, website, or organization in order to convince the network that they are supposed to be here. The hacker is meant to look like this other person so that the network will allow them through the security protocols and then the hacker can get through where they want, get the information that is needed, and even leave the system before anyone else is able to see them. There are a few options that you are able to pick from when it comes to the spoofing technique including:

IP spoofing

With the technique of IP spoofing, the hacker is going to mask up their IP address or make changes to it so that the network things that the hacker belongs to the network. The hacker is able to make these changes so that the IP address either matches up with what is allowed on the network or it is one that the network is going to be familiar with. With this method, the hacker is able to be in any part of the world that they want, but the network is still going to allow them to get on because the IP address matches up in some manner. Once the hacker is able to get on to the system, they have the ability to take over this network, change files, delete things, and do some other tasks without ever being detected.

If the hacker is able to pull off this technique, it is very successful because it has convinced the network that the hacker is supposed to be there. The trusted IP address is found by the hacker and then it is used to get onto the network and make the changes that are needed. The hacker will be able to use this in order to gain full access to the whole system, whether they choose to sit around and wait for a good opportunity or they choose to do an attack and get the information they want right away.

DNS spoofing

Another spoofing technique is known as DNS spoofing. This method is going to trick a user who is trying to get onto a legitimate site. The hacker will take the IP address and then when a user clicks on it, they will be sent to a malicious website where the hacker has complete control. Sometimes the hacker will take over a legitimate website and turn it to their use, but often they will change around a letter or two to trick people. Users who aren't paying attention or who type in the address wrong will be sent to a bad website and the hacker can take credentials and private information from the user.

Often the user will not realize that they are being tricked. They will get onto the website and figure that it is just where they want to be. They can put in private information, send payment, and more while the hacker is collecting it all privately.

For the hacker to get this to work, they need to have the same LAN as their target. This requires the hacker to search for a weak password on one of the machines that is on the network, something that is possibly even from a different location. Once the hacker accomplishes this, they will be able to redirect all users to their website and easily monitor the activities that are done there.

Email spoofing

Email spoofing is one of the most common types of spoofing, which is one of the reasons that people should be very careful about the emails that they are receiving, sending, and clicking on. This can be a useful technique when the hacker wants to try and get past some of the security that is placed on email accounts. Most email servers are going to be good at recognizing if someone looks like they are legitimate and when something is spam, but there are also times when the hacker will be able to get past this and can send malicious attachments.

The most common form of this is when the hacker is able to pretend to be someone else inside the system so that they can intercept the emails from both parties, either read them or make changes, and then send the emails on without

13

either of the two parties knowing. This can be really useful to the hacker because they can really get stuff done, and get ahold of private information that might be hidden elsewhere.

Phone number spoofing

When it comes to using phone number spoofing, the hacker is going to get ahold of some false numbers, or even area codes, so that they can mask their location. This is the best way for the hacker to be able to get into some of the voicemail messages that you have, and even to send out some text messages using this number. The target is often misled about where the hacker is from. Often this one is used when the hacker wants to pretend that they belong to a government office to trick the target.

The spoofing attacks can be difficult because often the network administrator is not even able to find out these attacks. The hacker will be able to stay on the network and cause almost as much damage as they want to these systems, without ever being found. It is often only after the hacker causes a big mess or when important information is leaked out that the hacker is finally caught and taken off the system. The hacker will be able to use just these kinds of hacks or some of the others in order to get the results they want and often they will be undetected by others on the same network.

Chapter 4: Man in the Middle Attacks

In addition to being able to do the spoofing attacks that we talked about in the previous chapter, it is also possible for a hacker to do a man in the middle attack. Sometimes the hacker will do this as a passive attack in order to just get on the system and see what information they are able to get, and other times they will use an active attack to get information, slow down the system, or cause some other form of problems.

When it comes to the man in the middle attacks, the hacker is able to do this with a form of spoofing that is called Address Resolution Protocol, or ARP. With this, the hacker is able to send messages that are false, but which are going to look normal, all over the network that they are working on. When it is pulled off, these fake messages allow the hacker to link up with another IP address of one of the users on the network. Once the hacker is done with this part, they can receive any of the data that all of the users are sending with this IP address and use it in the way that they would like.

So basically with this, the hacker is taking over an IP address and making it their own. They will receive all files, communication, and other information that is meant to go to the original user and they can use it however they would like. The hacker has the ability to get onto the network while receiving all traffic that goes on the network as well.

1. Session hijacking—this is when the hacker will use their false ARP to still the user's ID for the session. The hacker will be able to hold on to the information about the traffic and use it at a later date to get access to the account.

2. Denial of service attack—this is an attack done when the ARP spoof links several IP addresses to the target. During this attack, the data that should be sent to the other IP addresses are sent to one device. This is going to result in an overload of data.

3. Man in the middle attack—with this attack, the hacker is going to pretend that they are non-existent inside the network. Since they are hidden, they are able to modify and intercept messages that are sent between two or more users on the network. The one network may send a legitimate email, but the hacker will take it and change the information to be more

malicious before sending it on. The second user will open the malicious information, believing it to be safe.

Now that we know a bit more about a man in the middle attack, you are probably interested in learning some of the steps that are needed in order to complete the man in the middle attack. Here are some of the options that you can use and we are going to bring in the tool called Backtrack in order to get this done:

Do the research

The first step that you will need to do is find out the data that is needed to begin. The tool Wireshark is a good one to work with because it will help you to get all of this information to get on to the system. Firing up this tool on the network is going to allow the hacker to see what traffic is able to get onto the network through either the wireless or wired networks and is a really good place to get started for an access point.

Use your wireless adapter in monitor mode

Now that we have done some research, it is time to work with the wireless adapter and change it over to what is known as the monitor mode. This mode is going to make it easier for you to see the traffic that goes into your connection, even the traffic that isn't allowed to be there. This method is the one that you will work when using hubbed networks because you will find that the hubbed ones won't have as much security as you will find with the switched networks.

If you are able to see what information is going between the users that are on the switch, or you would like to make a bypass over this completely, you are able to work on making changes to the entries that are inside of your CAM table that is responsible for mapping out the IP and MAC addresses that are sending information to each other. When you are able to make changes to these entries, it is easier to get ahold of this traffic, make changes or at least read through it, and then send it back on without others knowing. The ARP spoofing attack is going to make this easier to accomplish.

Turning on backtrack

Now that you have changed the adapter and gotten it set up the way that you would like, it is time to fire up the Backtrack that you would like to use. You will need to pull up the Backtrack and then pull up all three terminals. Next, you will replace the MAC address from the target client with your personal MAC address. The code for doing this is: arpspoof [client IP] [server IP].

Once you do that, you will need to reverse the order of the IP addresses in the string that you just used. This is going to tell the server that your computer is the authorized one so that you are allowed to get onto the system and perform other tasks. You are basically going to become the server and the client so you can receive packets of information and change them how you wish. It also goes the other way around.

For those who are using Linux, you can use the built in feature known as ip_forward, which will make it easier to forward the packets you are receiving. Once you turn this feature on, you will be able to go back into Backtrack and forward these packets with the commandecho 1 >/proc/sys/net/ipv4/ip_forward.

This command is going to make it easier to be right between the client and the server. You will get all the information that goes between these two and as the hacker, you can use the information as you wish. You could look at the system, take personal information, or change anything you want about information that is shared.

Check out your traffic

At this point, you should be able to get access to all of the information that the users are all sending through the network. You will get to be right in the front row of this action and you can either watch the information that is being sent or grab ahold of some of it and make changes before sending it all back through the system again. You can use your BackTrack tool in order to sniff out the traffic and get a nice clear picture of the system. You need to take some time to activate this feature in order to make it work, but it can make things easier to work with.

Get your data as well as the credentials

Now you will just need to wait around and see when the client is logging into the server. Once the client logs on, you will be able to see their username and password coming up right in front of you. This means that the information is going to be right in front of you, making it easier to record and use it whenever you would like. Since the users and the administrators are all going to use these same credentials on all of the systems on the computer, you can keep using these credentials in order to get anywhere that you would like. You are now right in the middle of all the information on the system and you can use it in any manner that you would like, without other users on the system having any idea.

And now you are done creating your very first man in the middle attack. This is a great way for you to get in the middle of the all the action on a system, and the other users will have no idea that you are there. There are many things that you are able to do from here, such as intercepting information, changing the messages that are sent, slowing down the system, and even getting ahold of some classified information. this can really put the hacker right in the middle of the action so it is a great way for you to get started.

Chapter 5: How to Use Hacking to Get Passwords

The biggest target of hackers is to get passwords, mainly because they are really easy to get. Most people think that they just need to come up with a longer password in order to protect themselves, but there is more to it than that. If the hacker is able to use some of the tricks we stated earlier in this chapter, it does not matter how long your username and password is, they will still have it sent directly to them.

Confidential log in information, including passwords, are considered the weakest links in security because the only thing it relies on is secrecy. Once the secret is out, the security is pretty much gone. This is why it is such a big deal when a big company is hacked and all the username and passwords are leaked. The hacker is now able to get onto the system and use your information however they wish. Sometimes, the user themselves will inadvertently give out their own password for hackers to use.

So how do you hack a password? There are several ways that the hacker can do this including a physical attack, social engineering, and inference. There are also a few different tools that are used to crack passwords including:

1. Cain and Abel—this one is good to help with Windows RDP passwords, Cisco IOS hashes and more.

2. Elmcomsoft Distributed Password Recovery—this one is able to get PGP and Microsoft Office passwords and has been used in order to crack distributed passwords as well as recover up to 10,000 networked computers.

3. Elmcomsoft System Recovery—this has the ability to set administrative credentials, rest expirations on passwords, and reset passwords on Windows computers.

4. Ophcrack—this will use rainbow tables to crack passwords for Windows.

5. Pandora—this can be a good one to use to crack Novell Netware accounts either online or offline.

Some of these tools do have a shortfall because they will require the hacker to have physical access to the system they are hacking. But once the hacker has access to the system that you are protecting, they will be able to dig into all of your encrypted and password protected files with just a few tools.

Often, the hacker is not going to have access to your computer to do a password hack and they will rely on some other tools. Some examples of other methods used to hack a password include:

1. Dictionary attacks—these are attacks that will make use of dictionary words against the password database. This makes it easier to figure out if there is a weak password in the system.

2. Brute force attacks—these are capable of cracking all types of passwords because they are going to use all combinations of numbers, special characters, and letters until the device is cracked. The biggest flaw with this technique is that it can take a ton of time to uncover the password.

3. Rainbow attacks—these are good for cracking any hashed passwords. The tool is really fast compared to others, but it is not able to uncover passwords that are more than 14 characters.

4. Keystroke logging—this is one of the best techniques for cracking a password because it is asking the targeted computer to basically send over the information. The hacker is able to place a recording device on the targeted system to take in all the keystrokes done on the computer. The information is then sent over using programs such as KeyGhost.

5. Searching for weak storages—there are a lot of applications in computers that will store the passwords locally, making them vulnerable to a hacker. When you have physical access to the computer, it is easy to find the passwords through text searches and sometimes they are even stored on the application.

6. Grab the passwords remotely—often it is not possible to physically access a system, it is still possible to get the passwords from a remote location. You will need to do a spoofing attack first, exploit the SAM file and have the information sent to you.

Once the hacker has access to these passwords, it is easier for them to get the information that they want. They can use the passwords to get onto the network, to get to emails, find out financial accounts, and so much more. You must remember that passwords are a huge vulnerability in your system and to figure out more secure ways to protect your system.

Chapter 6: Getting Through Internet Connections for the Hack

If you would like to work on hacking online, you will need to learn how to get through the internet connection, as well as the security features, that are found online. Here we are going to talk about how to hack through a WEP connection as well as how to perform an evil twin hack so that you can check to see if your system is susceptible to this kind of attack or not:

How to hack a WEP connections

While there are a few different types of internet connections that you can work with in order to hack, this is one of the easiest to go through. If this is the one that your system is working with, you will definitely need to run through a few tests to see if you have been hacked or if you can make it more secure. Some of the things that you will need to check and hack through a WEP connection includes:

1. To get started, load up the BackTrack and the aircrack-ng. you can fire up BackTrack and then make sure that it is plugged into the wireless adapter to see if it is running. You can type in lwconfi in order to see if this is working. The program is then going to tell you which of the adapter it can recognize and if this is working properly, it is going to see yours.
2. Then take the wireless adapter and set it so it is at promiscuous mode. This will allow you to see what other connections are available and you can type in "airmon-ng start wlano" in order to do this. You can then change the name of your interface to have it read momo. You now have the adapter inside of monitor mode and you can type in "airodump-ng mono" to see which access points are available and what is attached to them.
3. Start capturing your access point. You will need to pick which connection you want to get on and then capture it. You can do this by using the command
   a. Airodump-ng –bssid [BSSID of target] -c [channel number] -w WEPcrack momo.
   b. Once you enter this command, the BackTrack is going to start capturing packets fro the access point on the right channel. This will

send the hacker all the packets that it needs in order to decode any passkeys that are present so they can get onto the wireless. However, it is important to realize that getting these packets will often take some time. If you need to get the packets quickly, it may be time to add in an ARP traffic.

4. Inject the ARP traffic—for anyone who doesn't want to wait around for the packets from WEPkey capture, doing an ARP packet and having it replay can help you get the packets that you need to crack the WEPkey. Since you already have the MAC and BSSID address from the target thanks to doing step 3, you will be able to use them to enter the following command:

   a. Aireplay-ng -3 -b [BSSID] – [MAC address] mono

   b. This will allow you to capture the ARPs through the access point of the target. You must keep going in order to capture the IVs that will come in as well.

5. Crack the WEPkey. Once you have the necessary amount of IVs in your WEPcrack file, it is time to run your aircrack-ng. Put in the command:

   a. Aircrack-ng [name of file]

   b. The aircrack-ng will enter the passkey in a hexadecimal format. You will just need to apply this key into your remote access point and then you are on the program. You can use it for free internet, to take over a computer on the system, and much more.

The Evil Twin Hack

The evil twin hack is an access point that will act like the access point that a user connects to, but it is manipulative. The target will just see their regular access point and think it is safe to get on, but this manipulative access point is used by a hacker to send the target to the hackers' premade access point, where the hacker can then start a dangerous man in the middle attack.

As a beginner hacker, you may need some practice doing the evil twin attack. Some basic steps to try out include:

1. Turn on BackTrack and start the program airmon-ng. Check to see if your wireless card is running properly by entering bt>iwconfig.

2. Once you have the wireless card, it is time to put it into monitor mode. You will be able to do this by entering the command bt >airmon-ng start wlan0.

3. Now you need to fire up the airdump-ng. you will start capturing the wireless traffic that your wireless card is able to detect. To do this, enter

the command bt >airodump-ng mono. After this step, you will have the ability to see all access points that are in range and can pick out the one that belongs to your target.

4. You will need to wait for when the target connects. Once the target gets onto the access point, you can copy the BSSID and the MAC address that you want to hack into.

5. Now the hacker will need to create an access point that has the same credentials.

   a. First, pull up a new terminal and type in bt > airbase-ng -a [BSSID] –essid ["SSID of target] -c [channel number] mono

   b. This is going to create the access point that you want. It will look the same as the original access point so the target will click on it, but it puts the hacker right in the middle as the one in control.

6. De-authenticate the target—for the target to get onto your new access point, you will need to get them off the one they are connected to. Since many wireless connections will go with 802.11, everyone who is connected to the access point will be de-authenticated when you do this. When the target tries to get back on to the internet, they will connect automatically to the one with the strongest signal, which in this case will be your manipulated access point.

   a. To get the target off their access point, make sure to do the following command: bt > aireplay-ng –deauth 0 -a [BSSID of target]

7. Turn the signal of the evil twin up. The trick on this one is to get the fake access point to have a strong signal. It needs to be at least as strong, but preferably stronger, than the original point of access. This can be tricky because you are likely further away than the original access point.

   a. Iwconfig wlano txpower 27 will help you to turn up the signal on your access point.

   b. This can add 500 milliwatts to your power. If you are too far away though, this may not be enough. You either need to be closer to the target or consider a newer wireless card that is able to go up to 2000 milliwatts.

8. Put the evil twin to good use—once you have established the evil twin and you know that the target and the network are all connected to it, it is time to take the steps needed in order to detect all the activities going on in the system. It often depends on what you want to do with the system for where you will go from here.

22

a. There are a lot of options of what to do at this point. Hackers who have gone and created an evil twin are interested in more than just free wireless so they will often do man in the middle attacks, intercept traffic, add in new traffic, or steal information from the system, often without the target realizing.

Conclusion

Working in the world of hacking can be really interesting. There are a lot of people who are interested in knowing how to protect their own systems from a hacker getting on and finding out information that they shouldn't, but most of us assume that going through the process of hacking is going to be too difficult to get started. But with the help of this guidebook, we are going to be able to learn some of the basics of working in hacking and how to protect your own network easily.

Inside this guidebook, we spent some time talking about the different ways that you are able to work with hacking. We started with some of the basics of hacking, such as the differences between white hat hackers and the black hat hackers and discussed how they often use some of the same methods to get things done. In addition, we talked about working on mapping your attack so that you have a plan and how to work with spoofing, man in the middle attacks, password hacks, and even how to hack through different connections online. All of these can come together to help you understand how to do a good hack and keep things safe from a hacker.

It is important that you learn how to keep your information safe from others who will try to get on your network and steal it. This guidebook is going to teach you some more about hacking and how you can use it for your needs and to keep your computer system safe.

Book 2

XML Crash Course

By: PG WIZARD BOOKS

Step by Step Guide To Mastering XML Programming!

Table of Contents

Introduction

When it comes to getting into the world of coding and all the programming that you would like to do, there are many options that you are able to choose from. Some choose to work with options like Java and HTML so that they can create projects online and on web pages that really wow. Others like to go with Python because it is an easy one for beginners to work with. But a great coding language that you can learn to work with and which we are going to discuss inside this guidebook, is the XML coding language.

You will notice as you go through this guidebook that there are some similarities that come up between the XML language and the HTML language. While both of these are similar, there are some differences that come up and we will talk about these inside of this guidebook. We will also spend some time talking about some of the basics of XML, some of the parts that you would want to add into the code to make things easier, how to declare XML documents (which is something optional you are able to do to make the code work a bit better) and even how to work with the different character entities to help make coding easier. These are just a few of the things that we will discuss in order to get you familiar with the XML code so that you can use it on your own.

When you are ready to get started on a new coding language and you want to pick one of the very best that is also easy for beginners to work with, you should learn how to use XML. This guidebook is going to give you the best results to ensure that you will learn everything that you need to know in order to start with the XML language.

Chapter 1: What is XML Programming?

When it comes to learning a new programming language, there are so many choices and it can all seem a bit overwhelming. You want to make sure that you are picking choices that will get you ahead and will make it easier to work on the systems and programs that you want, but with all of the choices that are out there, how are you going to be able to choose the one that is right for you. There are choices for beginners and ones for those who want to be a bit more advanced. There are choices that are great for working on websites while others are good for a specific operating system or for working inside of your business statistics. There really isn't a right or wrong answer, you just need to take the time to look at the different options and find the one that is right for you.

In this guidebook, we are going to take a look at the XML program. This one stands for Extensible Markup Language and it is one of the most talked about programming languages, only second to Java, because of all the great things that you are able to work with. inside of this language, you are able to store, organize, and identify your information with the help of tags. If you have used Java or JavaScript programming in the past, you may have heard about HTML tags, but these two are not quite the same. The XML language is not one that is going to replace HTML later on down the road, but it does introduce some new possibilities because it uses some of the features of HTML.

So, to make this easy, the XML program is going to be software and hardware independent and it is often used in order to carry information. even though the markup that is used will look similar to what you are finding with HTML, you will see that these are two different entities. For example, XML is set up to focus on the data that you are using while HTML is more focused on the appearance of your data. XML is going to describe your data while the HTML is going to display the data when you are done.

To make this work better, let's take a look at a good example of how this will work. Keep in mind that you will need to define some of your own tags because these are not predefined inside of XML. Here is the example:

<note>

```
<to>Jane</to>

<from<John</from>

<heading>Memo</heading>
```
<body>Come to the meeting at ten in the morning tomorrow</body>

</note>

With this example, you are probably able to tell what is going on. The information is there for both the sender as well as the receiver and there are headings and a body message that you will be able to use. But remember that the XML document is basically going to contain the information that you want along with some tags. There are no specific functions that go with it. On its own, XML is going to be pretty useless until you get the right software program in there to turn it into something.

Now basically, you are going to have three characteristics that come with the XML language that you are able to use and you can remember these by thinking about the name of the program. The three characteristics that you can work with include:

Extensible: this means that the XML program is going to allow you the change to characterize your own tags so that they will work with your application. You will also be able to extend the concept of the document, which is usually a file that is going to live on the server. It can also be a piece of data that is temporary and will flow between the various web servers.

Markup: this it eh elements or the tags that are familiar inside of XML. The elements that you are creating in this language will be similar to the ones in HTML, but you will be able to define the elements or tags that you want.

Language: the languages that are used inside of HTML and XML are pretty similar, but there is some more flexibility when using XML. You are able to use it to create and define some other languages rather than just having it set in stone like HTML.

Do I really need to learn how to use XML?

XML Crash Course: Step by Step Guide To Mastering XML Programming!

Many people wonder if it is worth their time to learn how to use XML since it is so similar to what you will find in HTML. You do need XML because there are times when you would like to create and deal with the data. The HTML document is just going to display the information; it is not going to work with it to make it look nicer or anything else.

In addition, working with XML allows you to use different contexts that are not just found on the web, including applications and web services. Any time that you would like to organize your data and send it over to another person, without having to worry about all the displays like you would find with HTML, the XML language is going to be the one to work with.

Downloading the XML language

Before we go any further in this guidebook and learn how to write some codes (as well as some of the other cool things that you are able to do in this language), we are going to need to take some time to get all of this downloaded onto the computer. The XML language is from Microsoft and at the time of this book, the XML Parser 3.0 is the option that we are going to use for our projects.

First, you need to make sure that the operating system and computer are the right kind to run this. To work with the XML Parser 3.0, you will need to have a Windows computer that is Windows 2000, Windows Server 2003, or Windows XP. You can then go to the Microsoft website to find this version, or a newer version, of the XML program an download it to your computer. Read through the prompts that come up on your screen until you get don with the download and it is all installed on your computer. At this point, you are ready to get started with some coding!

Chapter 2: Learning the Basic Syntax of XML

Now that we have the right program on our computer and ready to go, it is time to learn a bit about the syntax of a code in XML. If you learn the basic syntax of your code, it is going to be much easier to write more complex codes later on. Of course, with the options that we are going to talk about in this chapter, we are going to keep things pretty simple to start, but as you learn more about XML, it is pretty easy to add in the other parts that you will want to learn.

Below we are going to write out a basic syntax that you are able to use in this language and then we will take some time to discuss the different parts so that is makes sense for what you are doing. Here is the basic syntax that you can use:

```
<?xmlersio="1.0^)>
<contact-info>
<name>Manny Dunphy</name>
<company>Real Realtor</company>
<phone>(895) 444-1111</phone>
</contact-info>
```

As you can see with this example there are several parts of information that are placed inside. You need to make sure that the right syntax is used and the right symbols, so that the compiler has an idea of what you would like to send. This is a pretty simple option that will have the contact information for this person, Manny Dunphy, who works with Real Realtor as well as their phone number. You can expand this out as much as you would like or keep it this simple.

Remember than when working in XML, we are concentrating on the data, and collecting the data, rather than worrying about how the data is going to look. If you plan on putting this kind of information into a website or you want to make sure that it looks nice, you are going to need to work with the HTML format to make this happen.

XML Crash Course: Step by Step Guide To Mastering XML Programming!

Working with XML declarations

When it comes to XML, there are some documents that are going to have declarations and some that will not. If your document is one of them that has the declaration, here is a good example of how you would want to write it all out:

```
<?xmlv version="1.0" encoding="UTF-8"?>
```

For this one, the version is going to be the XML version and the other specific encoding is going to tell the document that you are going to use character encoding for this particular project. As we go through some of the other parts that you are able to work on in this book, you will see some more of the XML declaration and it is going to make a bit more sense to you.

Tags and Elements

Next on the list to work with are the elements and tags. The elements inside of XML are basically going to be the building blocks. They are going to be like a container that will hold many of the different parts of the XML ode, including media objects, attributes, elements, and text. Pretty much any element that comes into the code could be placed into the containers here. Each document is going to contain at least one element, but often there will be more if the code is longer. You can use the scopes in order to delimit using a start or end tag. Here is a good example of how you would write out the syntax for the elements and tags:

```
<element-name attribute1 attribute2>
...content
</element-name>
```

The element name in this example is the name that you would give to the element in this place. The name needs to be the same and matching in the beginning as well as in the ending tags. The attribute1 and attribute 2 are the element attributes that are going to be separated by some white space. You will be able to use the attributes in order to refer to a property of the element and often it is going to be associated with not only a name inside the code, but also with a certain value that you assign.

Writing out a comment inside of XML

There are times when you would like to leave a little comment inside of the code. When it comes to coding, the comments are just messages that the compiler is going to skip over and not read, but which can be useful to you or the other programmers who would like to go through the code. You will find that the syntax for writing out comments inside of XML is going to be the same as doing so in HTML. You will be able to use this syntax in order to write out your comment:

<!—An example of a comment→

Comments will need to all be done in this manner to tell the compiler when to start and stop the comment. When the compiler sees this, it will just skip over to the next part of the code, without causing any delays or issues in the code. You are able to add in as many of these comments as you would like or feel that you need in the code to make things easier, but you should be careful to not add in too many or you will end up with a messy code.

Starting a new line inside of XML

There are times when you will want to get started on a new line in XML. When it comes to doing this in applications of Windows, the new line is going to be done with the carriage return and line feed. On the old MAC systems, the new line is going to be with the carriage return and in Unix it is going to be the line feed. But when you are using XML, this is all going to be done with the line feed. You are able to start a new line in the code when you need to keep things in order and to make it easier to read through the code.

Unlike what you are going to find with HTML, the XML code is going to see white spaces a bit different. While you are able to have several whitespaces in a row on HTML, you will not have this inside of XML. Instead, if you have more than one whitespace in a row, the XML program is going to take these and turn them into just one.

These are just some of the basics that you are able to use when it comes to working in the XML coding language. They are going to help you to form some of the basics of your code and can come in use later on when you are ready to write out some more complicated codes. Make sure to learn some of these basics to make it easier for code writing later on and to further understand how the XML code will work for you.

Chapter 3: Declaring Inside of XML

We discussed the XML declaration a bit earlier on, but now we are going to break this down a bit in order to help it make more sense for you to use. The XML declaration is going consist of the details that you need to put in order by an XML processor to break down and analyze the document of XML. This is an optional feature that you can choose to either use or not use, however, when you do choose to use it, you will notice that it occurs right at the beginning of the document. Here is the syntax that you can use for XML declaration to make things a bit easier to use.

<?xml

      Version="version_nmuber"

      Encoding="encoding_delcaration"

      Standalone="standalone_status"

?>

Each of the parameters that you are going to use will have their own name so keep these in line and then an equal sign as well as a value. You are able to set up the numbers, rather than the quotes, to get the code to react in the way that you would like. There are a few rules that you will need to keep in mind when you are declaring inside of XML and these rules include the following:

- If there is a declaration inside of XML, you will need to make sure that you position it as the first line in your document. If you put it somewhere else inside of the document, you are going to run into some issues.
- When working with a declaration inside of XML, you will need to have a version number attribute to help make it work.
- The names and the parameter values that you set are going to be case sensitive, and it is recommended that while working inside of XML you keep the names in the lower case.
- There is a proper order that you are going to use with the parameter name to ensure that the compiler will read it properly. The proper order includes

version, encoding, and then standalone, just like you will see with the example that we gave above.

- You get to choose the quote type that you use, either the single or the double quotes. Just make sure that this stays consistent in the code.
- You will also notice that in this declaration, you will not need to have a closing tag like you do in some of the other coding that you will work with.
- If you are doing an encoding declaration, this is going to be a bit different, but for the rest of the declaration, you will need to keep it all in lower case letters.
- If you find that there are attributes, entities, and elements that are referenced or defined by an external DTD, your standalone is going to equal "no".

So now that we know a few of the rules that go with XML declaration, let's take a look at how you would do this in the code to get a better feel for it. This example is going to have all of the parameters defined for us.

<?xml> version='1.0' encoding='iso-8859-1' standalone='no'?>

And that is all there is to declaring inside of XML. Any time that you would need to do this inside of your code, you can just use this simple syntax, and then add in the information that you would like inside. This makes it easy for you to get the results that you want and as you can see, this only takes up about a line of code (maybe a little more depending on the declaration that you are using) and then you are all set.

Chapter 4: Working with Character Entities and Comments in XML

We talked about comments and some of the characters that you would use in XML a little bit before, but now we need to take this a step further and start to work on how the comments and the characters are going to work when it is time to actually write the code that you would like. When it comes to working with comments inside of XML, you will notice that they are similar to the comments that you have in HTML. They are basically little notes that are added into the code that will help you and other programmers to understand what is going on in the code, but will have absolutely no effect on how the code will work when it runs. One thing to note when writing out a comment is that you shouldn't try to nest one comment inside of another, because this will just cause a mess and could bring up an error inside of the code. Here is an example of a code that would have a comment in it (take the time to write this in your compiler to get some good practice).

```
<?xml version="1.0" encoding="UTF-8"?>
<!--Test scores are uploaded by grade -→
<class_list>
        <student>
        <name>Lilly</name>
        <grade>B+</grade>
        </student>
        </class_list>
```

Of course, this is a pretty simple example that just has one student and it is likely that you would add in a few more to fill this out but it is a good look at how the comment would be able to work inside of the code. It explains that the test scores were going to be upgraded by the grade that you were using and since we only used one it was not the most important, but if you had a lot of other students in here, it would show up. Remember that you are able to add in as many of these comments as you would like, you just need to be careful about using the right symbols to tell the compiler what you are doing.

Character Entities

The entity of the XML document is going to be the root of the entity tree and it is really the starting point for the processor. It can also be seen as the placeholder. The entities are going to be acknowledged being in the document prolog or in the DTD and they will often work with symbols that are only used for the entities and never for the content inside the code. For example, the < and > symbols are only used for the closing and the opening and the character entities are going to be used to make these visible.

Types of character entities

There are a number of character entities that you will be able to use inside of your code including the following:

Predefined character entities

These character entities are going to be introduced in order to prevent the ambiguity that can come when certain symbols are used. For example, there could be some issues when the (<) and (>) symbols are used along with the angle tags of (<>). The character entities are going to help delimit tags. You are able to use some of the following tags in order to get the right results in your code without showing all of the ambiguity at the same time:

Greater than: &gt

Less than: &lt

Ampersand: &amp

Single quote: &apos

Double quote: &wuot

Numerical character entities

With this entity, we are going to use numbers in order to reference and define the character entity that we want to use. We are able to choose numbers that are in decimal and hexadecimal format. There are lots of numeric references that you are able to use, and sometimes there can be too many for you to remember. The numeric reference is a number that is found in the Unicode character set. The syntax that you are going to be able to use for the decimal number reference inside of XML includes:

&# decimal number.

And then when you would like to use the hexadecimal reference, you would go with the following syntax:

&#x Hexadecimal number

Named character references

Wile the numerical character entities are a great way to get started, remember all of these numbers can be really hard, especially as a beginner who is just getting started with coding. This is why most people are going to use the name character entity instead to make things a little easier. There are a number of different ways that you can name the actions that you want to do inside of your code with the name character references, but here are a few of the examples that you can try:

- Acute: this one is going to refer to a capital A character that will have an acute accent on it.
- Ugrave; this is the name of the small u that has a grave accent.

Character entities and types are important when it comes to working inside of your code. They are going to help you to give the assignments to your work, whether you choose to use the numeric or one of the other choices. You can pick out the one that is right for you to work on your XML code.

Chapter 5: Processing and Encoding Inside Your XML Document

In this chapter, we are going to spend some time working on processing and encoding inside of your document. When you choose to work with processing instructions, you are allowing the documents to contain instructions for every application. You should know that these processes and the instructions are not going to be included in the character data that we talked about in the previous chapter, but they will still need to be able to pass through the application that you are creating.

The processing instructions will allow you to pass on the information that you would like to all of the different applications. You are able to place these in any location of the document that you would like. In fact, you are also able to place them into the prolog, which could include the document type definition or DTD, or at the end of the document as the textual content. The syntax to use in order to make this happen includes:

<?target instructions?>

For this syntax, the target is going to be responsible for recognizing the application from which the instruction comes from. You will be able to place the name of any application that you would like to use to tell the program where the instructions are located to use. And then the part of the instructions is going to be used in order to describe any of the information that you would like the application to process in order to finish it out.

The processing instructions are not used all that often because of the specialties that come with it. But if you do choose to work with these processing instructions, you will use them in order to link your XML document to a style sheet. In order to make this happen, you would need to type out the following type of syntax:

<?xml-stylesheet href= "businessforms.css" type="text/css"?>

These are basically the instructions that your target application is going to process inside of the XML document. With this particular instruction, the browser is going to be able to get the browser to recognize the right target by initiating that XML document and that it should transform it before it is shown. Notice that the first attribute comes out as the type of XSL that you are trying to transform and then the second attribute is going to indicate the location of the type you are transforming.

Working with XML encoding

Now that we have talked a bit about using processing inside of the XML document, it is time to work on the encoding inside of your documents. The process of encoding inside of XML is to convert the Unicode characters that you are trying to use into binary ones. The moment that the processor for XML reads a specific document, it is going to immediately encode the document according to the encoding type that you pick to go with it. There are different types of coding that you are able to use and we are going to look at them a bit more below:

Types of encoding

Inside of the XML code, there are gong to be two types of encoding that you are able to use, the UTF-8 and UTF16. They can both be used in separate ways in the coding that you work on. But if you end up not picking out the encoding that you would like to use with your XML document, the default is going to be the UTF-8. The syntax that you are going to use will depend on the type of encoding that you are using. For the UTF-8, you would use the following syntax:

<?xml version="1.0" encoding="UTF-8" standalone="no"?>

And then the syntax that you would need to use for the UTF-16 encoding would include:

<?xml version="1.0" encoding="UTF-16" standalone="no"?>

As you can see, these are going to be pretty similar, you will just put in the different options that you are able to use for the encoding. You will just need to pick the one that is best for you or choose to leave it blank so that the UTF-8 is going to be picked by default. Here is a good example of using the encoding of UTF-8:

```
<?xml version="1.0" encoding="UTF-8" standalone="no"?>
<contact-info>
        <name>Dunny Bobbins</name>
        <company>Real Realtors</company>
        <phone>(553) 512 1123</phone>
</contact-info>
```

With this example, we are using the UTF-8 encoding, as you are able to see by looking at that part of the code. This means that the 8-bit characters are the ones that you will use. For the most part, you would use this option when you want to have files that are encoded to be smaller because you are just going with 8 bits or smaller. If you don't care as much about the size of the file or you would like to get it to be bigger, the UTF-16 is going to be the option that you should use for your encoding.

And that is all there is to the encoding process. It is simple to use and will ensure that the document is going through the right processes to work properly. You can choose to go with either the UTF-8 or the UTF-16 based on your needs, but most of the time the UTF-8 is the best one to choose to go with and if you don't place an option into the code, you are going to find that the processor will choose to go with the UTF-8 by default.

Chapter 6: Working with the Elements and Tags

Earlier we spent some time talking about the elements and tags inside of the XML document, but we are going to now spend a bit more time on this to see how they actually work inside the code and how you can get them to work for your needs. When you are working inside of the XML program, tags are going to be one of the most vital parts. They are the foundation to your language because they are able to do so many things. You will be able to use them as a method to define the scopes of your elements, insert special instructions, declare settings necessary for parsing environments, and to insert comments. There are several different types of tags that you are able to use in XML and they are categorized by this:

Start tag

The start tag is the one that you will use in order to start all of the elements in XML that are non empty. You would be able to write it out similar to this: <address>

Empty tag

Another type of tag that you are going to use is an empty tag. In between the start tag and the end tag (which we are going to talk about soon), is the text that you are going to write out, or the content, of the code. If your element ends up not having any content, you will find that the tag is considered empty. There are a few ways that you are able to represent the empty elements that you are working with.

To start, if you would like to have an end tag that comes right after your start tag, you would just write it out like this "<hr> </hr>". You are also able to have an element tag that is completely empty such as writing out "<hr />". You are able to use these empty element tags for any of the elements inside of the code that aren't going to contain any content inside of them.

The end tag

In addition to the two types of tags that we have been discussing so far, you can also work with the end tag. This is just as necessary as working with the start tag because it tells the code when that particular part is all done or not. You would have a simple syntax to write out in order to make this happen, including </address>. This is going to be the complement to working with the start tag and you will need to have both of these in place inside of the code. Keep in mind that it will need to have the (/) symbol in front of it in order to prevent confusion and to help end out that part of the card.

Some of the rules for using tags in XML

Sometimes it can be a good idea to know the rules about the tags before you get too far into this process. This will help to speed things up and ensure that you are going to get the best results. Unlike some of the other languages that you will work with inside of coding, XML is going to be considered case sensitive. This basically means that you are going to have to take note and be careful when you are using upper case and lower case letters. The tags that you are creating inside of XML will need to be either all upper case letter or all lower case letters. You will find that a simple mistake in this field is going to give you some bad results, so always make sure to review each of the codes that you will use before finalizing them.

For example, if you typed into the code <address> and then ended it as </Address>, the code is going to have some troubles with these. The XML is going to see them as different because of the capitalization that comes with it, and it will start to treat this code as an erroneous syntax. In order to get this error fixed, you would have to change the ending tag so that it was lower case rather than the upper case that was used.

Another rule that you will need to keep track of when using your tags in XML is that you need to close them properly. For example, if you have a tag that is opened up inside of another element, you will need to make sure that it has been closed before the external element is all closed up.

When it comes to naming the tags that you will use, you need to be careful to get them the right way. For example, make sure that you are doing a good job of picking out the upper case and lower case letters and keeping them consistent when naming things is important. You also are not able to use any form of XML, regardless of the case that you are using, because it is going to confuse the processor and how it should behave. You can add in letters, digits, hyphens, underscores, and periods inside of the names of the elements. However, if you are using punctuation inside of this code, you are only able to use the underscore, hyphen, and period. The names of the elements are not able to have spaces. Outside of these simple rules, you are able to use any name that you would like to name the tags of your code.

Elements that are used in XML

Next on the list to explore are the elements that are inside of XML. The elements are kind of like the building blocks of the language, the part that is going to be built up on the foundation of the tags. These elements are great to work as containers that hold many things such as media objects, elements, attributes, and text and often they are going to hold many of these at once. Any of the documents that you work with inside of XML will have at least one of these elements, but the longer ones will hold more. For empty elements, the scopes will be delimited with the help of an empty element tag, but for the ones that have elements inside of them, the scopes are going to be delimited with the help of a start tag and an end tag.

Writing out the syntax of the element can be pretty easy, but here is a simple example to help you get it started:

<element-name attribute1 attribute2>

Whatever content you would like to add into here.

</element-name>

With the example above, the element name is going to be whatever name you would like to give the element in this case and then the attribute 1 and the attribute 2 are going to be the attributes that you give to your element, and they will be divided up with some white space. The attribute word is going to pretty much define the property of the element. It is going to work by associating the name back to the corresponding value, which is typically going to be a string of characters. When you would like to write out the attribute, you will simply write it out as name="value" and that is it.

When you are working on writing out the name of your element, take the time to see that the name you use in the start tag will be the same as the name that you place into the end tag. In addition, the word name should have an equal sign with it, as well as a string value that is inside of either double quotes or single quotes.

What about the empty element?

So above we were talking about a code that has an element inside of it. But there are times when you will have an empty element. Basically, the empty element is going to be an element that doesn't have content in it. When you are writing the syntax for this one, you would need to use the following format to tell the processor what to do:

If you are trying to create a new document and you will need to use a variety of elements, the following format is going to be the best:

<?xml version = "1.0"?>

<contact-information>

<address category = "home">

<name> Wendy Dawn </name>

<office> My Office </office>

<phone> (632) 246 1234 </phone>

<address/>

</contact-information>

Working with elements and tags inside of the XML document is one of the best things that you are able to do for your code. These are going to help you to get everything in place and they are the foundation and the building blocks that you really need inside of your code. It can take some time to learn the different things that you need inside of these, but when you are able to bring it all together, these are the two parts of the code that you need in order to really get it started the right way.

Chapter 7: Viewers and Editors in XML

Inside of XML, there are several methods that you are able to use in order to view documents. For example, you are able to use a browser in order to view a document, or you can choose to go with a simple text editor. Most of the browsers that are available will support XML, so this shouldn't be a worry. Or you can choose to just click on the files for XML and get them to open up; but remember that this is only going to work if the XML file is a local one. If the file is one that is found on your server, you just need to type in the right URL path into the address bar, just like when you want to open up some of the other files on your browser.

As mentioned, there are many ways that you are able to look and view the XML documents at any time that you would like and the method that you choose is going to be a personal decision. Some of the options include:

XML text editors: there are many text editors that you are able to use and you can make the decision that is right for you. Notepad, TextEdit, and Textpad are great options to work with to create and view documents in XML, but other options will work as well.

Google Chrome: while all browsers are going to work well with XML, this one is really good to work with. there seems to be few problems with using it and it makes it easy to open up the XML code you want to use.

Mozilla Firefox: this one is also a good browser to use, but you do need to first open the code in Google Chrome. To do this, you need to take the file and double click on it in order to see the code displayed in some colorful text. This is a good thing because it makes it easier to read the code. Then at the left portion of the element, you will see a plus and a minus sign. If you click on the plus sign, the code is going to expand but if you click on the minus sign, you will see that the code hides.

Errors in my document

There are times when there will be some errors in your XML documents. If you notice that the code is missing out on certain tags, there are some errors that are going to show up. If there is an error somewhere in the code, you are going to get a message that should contain some information about the error that you are dealing with. sometimes it is something simple such as misspelling a word or using lower case in the start tag and then upper case in the end tag. You will need to double check your code to see what the issue is so that you can make some changes to the code.

Editors in XML

When you are working inside of XML, you are going to need to work with an editor of some sort. The editor is going to be useful to create, as well as make changes, in the document that you are using. There are many different editors that you are bale to use and most of them are free and may even come on your computer already, so this can make things easier. For example, Notepad or Wordpad are two great options that you can use, or you can download a professional editor to use from online. The online editors are a bit more powerful and sometimes beginners like to go with them because they do some of the work, such as close tags that you leave open, check the syntax, and highlight the syntax in color so that it is easier to read. You can make the decision about what kind you would like to use and the features that you think will be the most helpful when you are learning how to code.

Conclusion

Working with a new coding language is something that can take some time and effort. You want to be able to get the most out of the language, but you also don't want to waste your time on something that is too hard to learn and understand. This guidebook is going to take a bit of time to discuss the XML coding language, how to use it and why you would want to learn this particular language.

Inside this guidebook, you are going to learn everything you need in order to do well with the XML code. We are going to start out with some of the basics that come with XML coding, such as what it is and how it varies from HTML (even though both of them are pretty similar) and then move on to some of the special parts that are found inside of your first code so that you can become more familiar with it all. Then we move on how you would declare inside of XML (which is something that is optional and you can choose to do or not) along with working in comments and special characters' amount other topics.

There is so much that you are able to do with the XML code once you take the time to learn this code and what all you can do with it. When you are ready to get started in coding or you are looking for a new code that you can work with, make sure to take some time to look through this guidebook and get the most out of the XML code.

www.ingramcontent.com/pod-product-compliance
Lightning Source LLC
Chambersburg PA
CBHW070902070326
40690CB00009B/1960